The Fourth Face of The Goddess

Gale Perrigo Hamby

Copyright © 2013 Gale P. Hamby

All rights reserved.

DEDICATION

TO MY PARENTS, LUCY & HARRY PERRIGO

MY FIRST GODDESS & GOD,
WHO GAVE ME MY PASSION FOR BOOKS,
WORDS AND THEIR MAGICK…
AND ALL I KNEW FIRST OF LOVE, HONOR,
AND COMMITMENT TO AN IDEAL.

THANK YOU.
YOU ARE LOVED ALWAYS.

What is the Fourth Face of the Goddess?

She is the Dark Moon, the opposite of the Full Moon.

Equal in power, Her time falls between the last light of the waning crescent and the first glimmer of the new crescent.

No light can be seen from the moon then; She is the hidden face.

As the Full moon illuminates, the Dark moon gives access to what cannot be seen at other times. She shows us the darkest pieces of our selves. The pieces we might fear to examine in the light... the pieces we keep hidden even from our own hearts in the light. The pain... the anger... the darkness we have accrued.

She is the Mother of 3 a.m.

In Her peaceful night, we can pull these out unafraid. There's no one here to judge. No one here to disregard. No one here to tell us to grow up, to move on, to get over it... no one here to tell us to stuff our pain away so that others don't have to watch us work through what hurts.

She accepts.

She understands.

She holds us in the deepest night and silently keeps us safe while we cry, or rage, or despair, until we pass to some kind of peace.

And then She lets us go on with life with a little lighter burden, until it's safe to look again.

May She bless and keep us all.

Gale Hamby
May 19, 2013

CONTENTS

	Acknowledgments	ix
1	Goddess and God	1
2	Short Stories	11
3	The Wheel	25
4	Longer Stories	39
5	Arcana	61
6	Never Again The Burning	73
7	Five Words for Love	87

ACKNOWLEDGMENTS

I offer thanks:

To my beloved husband Mike, whose
presence in my life engenders miracles…
and for accepting me just as you found me,
from the first moment we met.

To all my friends, for their endless support,
love and faith… especially Otter & Dan
(who saved my life), Alonnie, Idona,
and Gloria. I am blessed that you are
too many to fit all your names here.

Blessed Be, one and all.

With unending gratitude, I would also like to acknowledge the talented artists
Whose original works grace these pages:

Scott Bowden of Ravenfyre Designs – Cover Art, and Page 2

Heidi Carcano - Pages 4, 21, and 37

Michael Hamby - all Photographs

TempusBound Studio – Page X, 14, 42, and 94

CHAPTER ONE

GODDESS AND GOD

Raven, Raven

Raven, Raven, black as coal,
Glossy feathers, eyes so bold,
Tell me what the future holds...

Tell me what tomorrow brings,
Teach my captive heart to sing,
Show me all of everything...

Raven, guide my wings in flight,
Show me where my true path lies.
Guard me through the darkest night.

Change me with your trickster art-
Shift my shape to suit my heart,
Fear transforms to strongest part.

With thought and memory entwined,
Grant me power to unbind
The magick of my deepest mind...

Raven, lord of dark and bright,
Messenger, pray, here alight,
Prophesy my fate tonight...

Cowbirds

Cold sun and cowbirds
Fill my front yard. They're
Scorned by many, but I love them-
Flashy black suitcoats
And brown suede heads,

Their waterfall trills make me smile.
Greedy things, they hog the feeders
And stuff themselves
While more restrained birds watch in awe
And peck their cast offs from the grass.

We cannot all be cardinals,
Nor the bright blue jays
That swoop in like the fist of God
And sweep the others away before them
In a brilliant show of braggadocio.

I'm a fan of simple birds -
Sweet brown sparrows, humble finches-
Chickadees and titmice, all the
Wee feathered ones... these
Are what convince me that the Goddess
Sees and loves us all.

Triplicity

Part I - the Maiden

When I walked as the Maiden fair,
Naught existed I would not dare.
All worlds were my queendom,
All creatures, my friends;
Many the roads to all most rare.

And as I wished, my heart I shared-
Lovers I had, but did not forswear
My vows to myself:
To keep myself free,
Who seeks to cage me must beware!

My tread as light as morning air,
I walked where I would with little care;
I learned my own nature,
My weakness, my strength.
Light were the burdens I did bear.

Part II - the Mother

Then, as I grew older, the Mother's face I wore.
I raised many little ones, though children never bore...
My children were ideas, and words to tell the tale,
And fierce and strong my heart became.
I nurtured all my dreams and aims,
And kept them strong and hale.

In the swelling prime of life, I gave all without fear
The best of what I am went to those I held most dear...
Thus all the world became my child, to love, and guide, and guard.
But there were times I thinned the herds -
Pulled all the weeds, destroyed my words -

And those times broke my heart.

Wondrous joys and deepest pains...wisdom's price was dear,
But I have paid it gladly, as my path became clear.
I've loved and taught and created myself, and others too.
The ideals of my carefree youth,
Transmuted, by living, into truth,
Became what I chose to do.

Part III - the Crone

Then at last I became the Crone:
See my great disguise?
Behind the cheerful grandmama
The Ancient Dark does rise.
I am the crossroads' keeper,
Those roads that lead between...
Stern and wise, I know those things
That others call unseen.

What I know, I will share with those
Brave enough to ask.
The roads I've walked are perilous -
Are you equal to the task?
Not bound by love to answer,
Nor duty's relentless shout,
I challenge those who seek me now:
Do well, or do without.

Experience has tempered me.
Though the winds of change still blow,
Death holds no fearful mystery,
Nor does darkness lay me low...
No matter what my future holds,
I'll face it never alone,
For within me They still shine as one -
The Maiden, Mother and Crone.

The Fourth Face of the Goddess

Gracious Goddess, Dark and Bright,
Show me Your fourth face tonight...

Your other Faces ask too much.
They want results and plans and such -

The Maiden's eager joy for flight;
The Mother's lessons, choose wrong or right;
To dare the crossroads of the Crone -

Tonight, I'm wearied to the bone.
I seek a darkened place to rest
From this world's restless, aimless quests.

Tonight, I've not the strength within
To draw upon, to ease my pain.
I'll find the will to move tomorrow.
Tonight, let me confront my sorrow

In the safety of the dark.
Perhaps, in time, I'll find that spark
That put my feet upon Your path...
But now, the stars do naught but laugh.

I seek the refuge of Your hidden face
Until the endless stygian space
Is not so cold. And when that comes,
I'll find the strength to go back home.

A Blessing, for Lovers Separated

Fair Lady Moon, who walks the night,
Find my true love's eyes this night:
Let him know that he and I
Watch the same moon in the sky...
Fair Lady Moon, be ours tonight.

Gracious Goddess, an You love me,
Guard my love by land and sea.
Smile in perfect love on us;
I ask Your blessing in perfect trust.
Gracious Goddess, guard us, please.

Triple Goddess, in Your Aspects divine,
Turn my dear one's thoughts to mine,
As my thoughts always turn to his.
My thanks I give to You for this...
Triple Goddess, upon us shine.

Rises

She rises, oh! She rises
And the earth sings in flowers.
They bloom together.

Watchtower of the East

The tower stands at the edge of a meadow. The forest that borders it on three sides is green with new leaves, the new grass is vivid in the field. The rising sun, glowing just above the horizon, turns the tower pale shades of rose and gold, for its walls are as clear as glass, gleaming in the dawn. But do not think these walls fragile: they are made of diamond, and the roseate glow of the sunrise dazzles in the sheer, straight sides of the ethereal structure. It rises impossibly high and thin, a crystal shard piercing the white clouds as thought pierces the mind. The Lords that dwell and keep watch here are tall and fair, garbed in robes of the palest yellow-gold. Their eyes are kind, but sharp: they see everything, consider everything, weigh and measure everything as they seek the new beginnings inherent in all of life's movements, to inspire vision and hope in all who come to this place.

Watchtower of the South

The tower stands in the desert, at the edge of a deep canyon. It is plain and robust, sturdy, formidable. Its walls are the colors of the desert, pink and rose and garnet - all the hues of the stones beneath it, but chiefly these. It blends with the terrain under the baking heat of the noonday sun overhead. Waves of heat rise and shimmer in the air above the tower, and on these waves glide the nimble dragons, with their leonine manes and stained-glass wings, glittering in the sun as they soar on the thermals. The Lords that dwell and keep watch here, that ride these Steeds, are garbed in red, loose robes that reflect the searing heat of their domain. They appear young, like children, innocent as they laugh with the delight of their flight, but their eyes are fiery and filled with passion as the ceaselessly patrol their dry lands, seeking to do battle with any that challenge them, to ignite will and determination in all that pass their way.

Watchtower of the West

The tower stands on the shore of an endless sea. White and clean is the sand upon which it rests, that is washed by the waves of the warm and sonorous waters. The full moon is rising over these waters, her rays streaming to the base of the tower, that is caressed by the foam of the surf. The tower is all of coral, red, black and white, all blending together in the rounded sensuous shapes of shells. Shells cover much of the walls, in wild profusion of shapes and sizes. The windows are great scallop shells, through which a light shines softly. Great serpents sport among the gentle waves, and whales sing in the depths. The Lords that dwell and keep watch here wade along the shore in the moonlight. Their robes are all the colors of the water, and they wear masks of blue, beaded with pearls. Their eyes do not judge. They see deep within the souls of all who come to this shore. The peacefulness of their nature radiates from them, so that all who venture here, whether from pain or joy, find healing or laughter, and safe harbor from the storms of their hearts.

Watchtower of the North

The tower stands black and stark amid the crags of the ancient mountains. Here the oldest roots of the world dig deep into the earth. Here the bones of the earth lie close to the surface. The light of the waning crescent moon slides down the adamantine walls, that are studded with all dark stones: onyx, smoky quartz, black moonstones. The wind mourns among the spires, clouds scud across the sky, and over all hovers the sense that time has fallen away, and exists not at all in this place of perfect solitude. Yet there is a sense of impending change, as if this is a crossroad in the center of the Universe. The Lords that dwell and keep watch here are almost silent in their dark robes, speaking in whispers, observing all that passes with glittering eyes. Nothing escapes their sight, as seekers come to the great black iron gates to find the strength to endure the road they must walk, or the death of the old to find a new path.

CHAPTER TWO

SHORT STORIES

Blacksnake

I invoke Thee, o Great Blacksnake of the night:
Come, I will coax you close
With the live rats of my tangled thoughts.
Coil about me, sleek and shielding,
For I am weary and there is no anodyne.
No sun nor friend nor heart's ease can equal
Thy cold glowing eye, like the moon,
That looks so deeply into mine...
Consume me, soul of darkness,
That I may rest in peace.

Faeries

Tiny faeries snarl
In the peony garden.
My heart is amazed.

Little Animals

Because those wee ones,
Being wounded, cannot pass
The Gates by themselves...

We act to aid them,
Their small souls given to us-
Kindness hurts them less

Than what has brought them
To our doorsteps, as it leaves
Our own hearts broken...

A grace we cannot
Give ourselves - and we bear it
For their own small sakes.

Cave

I want a cave to live in.
Dark as sleep
Cool as dreams
Deep as forever.

Where
Hiding is encouraged
And the light comes
In only so far.

I want a cave to live in.
Water flows
Softly through
My living room.

Where
Small animals creep
In to drink and
Rest themselves safe.

I want a cave to live in.
Self-contained
Earth-sheltered
Ecologically sound

Where
I creep out
To forage and return
To nest among dried leaves.

I want a cave to live in.
Safe as the night sky
Peaceful as the moon
Quiet as the grave.

secret heart

You
blaze black
lightning in my
secret heart.
Welcoming,

I
receive as
the earth receives
the rains
falling...

Drink
in that
Darkness that is
the heart
you

show
no one.
I am darkness
at the
core

and
call out
to you, seeking
the light
hiding

in
us both
that loves the
night as
truth.

Until The Morning

And when the true Night falls,
And in that seamless black the endless glare of
What has hidden lain is now aroused...

What solace can I seek, what shelter
Will avail me respite?
Stumbling through the shrouds,

When all light fails,
When even stars their timeless glows snuff out...
When blind eyes wide find blackness over all...

Then your spirit beacon-like will guide me,
Shine me home across the shoals of what has been,
Is now, and what will come.

And over all the ages, and the miles,
And the dreams forsaken,
We will hold hands in the dark until the morning.

Connecticut

You
Who act
Fate's agent in
This mad
World...

Your
Thread is
Tied to mine.
The murdered
Ones,

The
Ones I
Love, all threads
Of the
Same

Tapestry.
Amidst despair,
Hope rises that
Someday we
Somehow

Will
clearly see
that Fate cuts
all threads
with

The
Same knife.

For Stephanie

Heart's blood, she will not
Be forgotten - she will be
Reborn to us in love.

(Written for my friend Silverhand Hawke,
whose beloved daughter Stephanie
passed from our midst in April, 2012…)

For Andrea, at 13, With Regret

Little girl,
You are like the duckling
      in that ancient tale,
But no Swan waits
In your wings to enter -
Fairer by far, Falcon flies
      out of your angry eyes...
But only a fledgling
Seeking the sky before its time.
You are so bold - so young -
Can you be but a child
Yet a bit longer,
That your wings can reflect
The sun like lightning,
      and not the blaze
Of Icarus, falling, falling?

Hole

She says,
"there is a hole

right

here," and her palm
against my chest is burning,

"and nothing fills it.

Not food, not love, not learning.

Just a hole, and the night
Within it more
Than I can bear sometimes."

And in her eyes, locked onto mine,
I see such darkness, an empty chasm
That spawns such flights of
Dismal fancy, that I am laid waste
By her despair, and I reach out
To her and touch

the mirror

Pendulum

Tonight the past
Is so present
That the future disappears.
This will pass, they said.
This will swing back
The other way soon.

They said.

I have shoved that pendulum
So hard the other way
That it broke.
Pieces of it jam
The doors of my memory,
Wedging them wide,
Despite my efforts
Not
To
Look
Inside.

Just move along,
Nothing to see here.
Nothing but little
Dusty bags that wrap
The pieces of my heart
I thought gone for good -
But only stored
Against a moment
Of weakness.

Dragons' Wings

Would I had the wings
Of dragons; bear me up and
Fly from here. My heart

Distrusts my mind to
Save me, and it seeks to flee.
I feel the weight of

Years upon me. Sick
Of commonplace, I yearn for
Wings of flaming gold

To lift me up from
Too-full world to empty realm
Of peaceful darkness,

Quiet, cold, and safe,
Away from puzzles rending, harsh,
Impossible to solve.

I'd weep no more with
Wings of dragons...bear me up
And far from here. My

Heart seeks solace in
The night. I'd leave my pain in
Flames behind me then...

CHAPTER THREE

THE WHEEL

Winter Solstice – Yule

We come together by this hearth
A vigil for to keep:
To bring the Sun's light back to earth
We shall forsake our sleep
And in the darkness share our power,
Until the dawn's first shining hour.

With longest night the winter comes,
We contemplate the lost
Forgotten things that pulled us from
Our comfort - and the cost.
We find each other in the night
And share together our hard-won light.

With holly, oak and mistletoe
Our circle is made bright.
The Yule log before us glows,
And in its cheerful light
We find the courage that we need
To plant the new year's fertile seeds.

And so, with family, lovers, friends,
The Great Wheel slowly spins...
We praise the Light as darkness ends,
And Sun's return begins.
The Balance is kept with Darkness and Light...
Pray peace to you all, and to all, a good night!

As Imbolc Comes Again

Find the Lady 'neath the snow,
Round and round the fire go!
Feel the light begin to grow,
As Imbolc comes again.

Hear the forge with hammers ring -
Brighid crafts the promise of spring..
Feel the earth begin to sing,
As Imbolc comes again.

The Goddess from the dark has come,
So light the lamps, make bright your home,
Welcome the Maiden who was the Crone
As Imbolc comes again.

A crown of candles upon Her brow
Lights the way for seeds to grow,
And new life blooms above the snow
As Imbolc comes again.

Spring Equinox -The Goddess & the Moon Hare

The Moon Hare said to the Goddess at dawn,
"Tell me, Lady, will spring be long?
I want the snow to be on its way,
So my tribe and I can frolic and play
In the meadows all freshly green."
Ostara said, "Wait and see."

"But, Lady," the Hare asked plaintively,
"The days grow longer, don't You see?
Soon they will equal the span of night,
And darkness surrender to the light,
And buds will return to the trees!"
Ostara said, "Wait and see."

The Moon Hare replied, "Remember when I
Was a dying bird, unable to fly?
For spring came late, and my wings froze-
I would not suffer again such woes!
Tell me when You'll come back to me?"
Ostara said, "Wait and see."

Bending, She took the Hare into Her arms,
"Think you I'd let you come to harm?
You went from bird to bonny March hare
For 'twas my doing that put you there -
Rest assured, I will come to thee,
You only need wait and see.

"Then flowers shall rise and the trees will bud,
And life surge forth with singing blood,
The grass grow green, and on that one day
It's given to you your eggs to lay,
For children to find - how happy they'll be!
I ask you, just wait and see."

And so, my loves, let us wait like the Hare:
The promise of Spring is in the air.
And in Her good time we'll see the change
From Winter's cold snow to Spring's soft rains.
The Wheel will turn, and blessed all will be
We need only wait and see...

Beltane

Run with me, love, to the wild wood,
To my shady hidden bower,
Where we may glimpse the bold young God
Courting His fair wild flower.
For the Maiden's abroad in Her glory
Beneath the moon aglow,
And wherever Her feet may take Her,
The God is sure to go.

Ah! See Her there, by the oak tree?
She shines with the moon's own light!
Sweeter than hive's first honey,
Fiercer than peregrine's flight.
As if sensing pursuit around Her,
She wheels toward the woods to go -
But the young God stands before Her,
Stars bound upon His brow.

There's naught of the child about Him,
Though born but short months ago -
He's strong and proud as a wild stag,
Unafraid of the Huntress' bow.
And Her free heart swells within Her,
Her eternal eyes meet His,
And the Wheel is turning about Them,
As They pledge Their troth with a kiss.

Come, love, let us leave Them
As we turn to each other's arms -
For the season's as full of promise
As the night is full of stars.
Around us, within us, the Wheel turns,
As your heart and mine both know...
The love of the Gods is sacred,
And as above, so below.

Summer Solstice - Litha

'Tis the dawning of the longest day,
And all the sun's light falls upon
The Goddess giving birth
As the Mother She becomes.

The glory of the Sun shines down
And brightens every hour spent
Beneath His golden rays-
Now the God is in His prime.

But from this night the light will wane
The Sun King will grow weaker
Until once more at Yule
He'll begin His journey back.

So celebrate this longest day, for
God and Goddess wed shall be
And He will pledge His life
To Her people and Her lands.

Let the fiery wheels roll down the hills,
Let scarlet ribbons deck the oaks.
Celebrate the bounty
Of the Earth in fruitful flower...

Let us leap the blazing bonfires,
Let us set the watch together!
Sing the praise of summer
With us on this longest day.

Lughnasadh - First Fruits

Hail to the God of many Skills!
Hail to Lugh, the Craftsman,
The Smith, the Bard,
Who grants us creativity!

The grain grows high, golden in the fields.
We have not harvested till now -
Skilled are our farmers,
Our last harvest has fed us till this day!

We go forth and bring down the grain.
This night, there will be bread,
Hot and fresh, and fruit from the orchards.
We are grateful for our abundance.

Hail to the God of many Skills!
Hail to Lugh, the Craftsman,
The Smith, the Bard,
Who grants us skillful hands!

We celebrate the first fruits,
The first harvest, with song and games,
And we honor the Goddess Tailtiu,
Who fostered Lugh and whose labors

Cost Her life - the grieving God
Did call for a feast in Her honor.
We come together to give Her praise,
Who gave Her people life in darkest times.

Hail to the God of many Skills!
Hail to Lugh, the Craftsman,
The Smith, the Bard,
Who grants us strong arms!

Today let us all come together
In tests of skill, to trade our goods,
To give praise to the Lord and Lady of Plenty,
That we may prepare for months ahead,

That we may see this season's bounty
Gathered in joy and shared in love,
Safely stored for the coming nights
To keep us hale and sound.

Hail to the God of many Skills!
Hail to Lugh, the Craftsman,
The Smith, the Bard,
Who grants us victory over darkness!

Fall Equinox - Mabon

Now is the season of the final harvest.
Light and Dark are equal.
The Horned One, Lord of the Sun
By His free will becomes the Lord of Shadows;
Lord of Dreams, His power will hold sway
Throughout the lengthening nights.
The fruits of the harvest must sustain us now.
As the Goddess retreats into the Earth,
She teaches us restraint.
As Light must have Dark to balance,
So must the bright summer
Embrace the winter to rest and be reborn.

Samhain - Trick or Treat

I put the big bowl of candy
By the front door... leave the light on
                                    Leave a plate of favorite foods
                                    on the altar.
                                    That light is always on. I open
                                    the door...

Little feet sound on the porch,
Giggles and excited chatter
                                    From the corner of my eye,
                                    A shadow, a flicker of
                                    movement.

The doorbell sounds,
Whispers of "Somebody's coming!"
                                    A shiver up my back, the sense
                                    Of someone standing near me,
                                    silent, waiting.

I open the door : a covey of little
Witches, pirates, princesses, clowns
                                    And out beyond the street
                                    light's glow
                                    Another stands, almost
                                    familiar

They hold out bags, in unison
Crying "Trick or Treat!"
                                    A trick of the darkness? Then,
                                    I am treated to a dear face from
                                    my past...

I toss in extra candy, handfuls each,
Their smiles grow amazed
                                    I hear your voice in my mind,
                                    kind and loving
                                    Your smile warms me as it
                                    always did

A chorus of gratitude trills
Around me and a swirl of colored silks

                          I raise my hand to you - I see
                          you wave back,
                          The night swirling around
                          you, too soon, too soon

As the flock departs in a rush
Of sugared joy to seek more booty

                          And I want to cry, "Don't go!
                          Don't go!"
                          But I know you and the rest
                          will be always near me...

                All my beloved dead,
                While the Veil is thin

CHAPTER FOUR

LONGER STORIES

A Bardic Lay

Come, gather round, maidens, and give me an ear:
Of the wandering harper, you need feel no fear.
In winter and summer, he travels the land
His harp o'er his shoulder, his staff in his hand.

A bard came to camp with us one summer night
His smile was merry, his hazel eyes bright...
Wore a Druid's white robes, but he said with a glance
That he might be coaxed out of them, given a chance.

As he played by the fire, I studied his hands,
Long-fingered and sure on the harp's silver strands;
How lucky the woman caressed so would be...
I determined that woman, tonight, would be me.

So I sat by his side and I passed him the wine,
And as he took the bottle our fingers entwined
The look in his eyes made me weak with desire
And he smiled as we walked away from the fire.

The forest was peaceful as a blanket I spread.
He lay down beside me and I gave him his head
As a rider should do with a high-blooded steed...
The quiet woods echoed with passion and need

Until dawn stole upon us. Reluctant, we stirred,
And we rose and we dressed with scarcely a word,
For our smiles said more than mere words could convey
As we strolled back to camp while the mist cleared away.

And I'll never forget the sweet blaze of that night,
Though many a year has, by now, passed me by...
And the secret I treasure, and will never disclose,
Is exactly what Druids wear under their robes.

Patience

If, in among the tangled skeins
Of our lives lived in ages gone,
One silver thread may still be found
Of one we loved, and with whom belonged -
Then, having this thread to love and trust,

Might we not bear our current place
With patience, and a certain grace?
And know that we have but to wait
For this brief span of time to pass
(a moment only, as aeons go)
Until we meet, this clue in hand,
In another time; and recall and know
The beloved one, in whose embrace
The pact was sealed: to live and teach
And learn and love this life and more,
Bound then together, each to each.

Have we remembered and known before,
As we know now, of this ancient tie?

How can this life be the only one
When we know why our hearts heard only lies
In what others said of what we must do
To fit the mold of a happy life?

And aye, I know it seems unfair
As we swim upstream in a river of strife,
That this thread we cling to, to stay afloat,
Must be cast aside for a shadow's kiss...
But be still, my heart, and remember this:

Love is an arrow straight and true,
Flung from the string of a silver bow -
There is much may happen we cannot know.
Hold fast to the knowing of what has been,
And know, in your heart, it will be again.

Daemon Lover

He comes to my chambers many a night,
Whether Lady Moon be dark, or bright...
His words as sweet as fruit just ripe,
He must be my daemon lover.

I'm thought a good woman, a blessing to all,
With stalwart husband and a fine hall -
Yet still his advances hold me in thrall,
My handsome daemon lover.

For duty and fortune, my place is here.
And I love my doughty lord most dear -
But my soul will lie forever elsewhere,
With my princely daemon lover...

I'll feel his breath upon my ear
As he whispers charms only I can hear.
He makes me quiver, but not with fear,
Does my darksome daemon lover...

He speaks me sweet, he tups me fair,
His kisses whisk away all my cares.
No mortal paramour half compares
With my skillful daemon lover.

When morning comes, I rise and go
About my tasks, but well I know
That when sun sets and moonrise glows,
I'll see my daemon lover.

And one day, perhaps, if the gods do will,
When time and space do both stand still,
When vows and duty both be fulfilled,
I'll go with my daemon lover...

Over those dark hills so far away,
There waits my daemon lover.

Reply (with Apology to John Keats)

Loitering alone and pale,
How boring to be a human male!
To think thy kisses should to thee bring
The privilege of clipping elfin wings!
Be happy I gave thee what thou got:
So many others have shared me not!
I know what ails thee, Knight-at-arms -
Thine attitudes have done thee harm.
Thy Holy church with its wedded bliss
Has nothing that compares with this!
I thought to please thee and myself
By giving thee tastes of faerie wealth.
That thou enjoyed it, thou didst prove -
But to sit here now, and cry of love?
No birds do sing, thou selfish lout,
Because thy wailing drowns them out!
So if thou shouldst name me sans merci....
The fault, I fear, doth lie with thee.

Dream

This is the quiet dream:

We sit together on the biggest boulder.
My feet still dangle; your wings brush the grass,
Glossy midnight in the setting fire of the sun.
You do not wear these in our daytime world,
Only here, in this place of constant twilight,
The moon just rising always, the night never quite come.
Time is strange here, and yet your face is not.

Yew branches behind us rustle in the breeze.
Small winged shapes kite up, down.
Your eyes follow, amused at their antics,
And I wonder if you will join them
Or sit here still, kind to my earthbound form.

"The heart wants its own," you murmur, "and
Seeks its own down misbegotten roads
We can follow only at our peril.
And yet, follow we do."

"The mind," I answer, "knows all the reasons
Why we should not go.
It tells the heart those things.
Part of us seeks reason."

I shiver in the cooling air, and
You wrap your wing about me.
We hold hands in the sheltering softness.
Your lips brush my ear as you whisper,
"And yet, the heart sings. The mind speaks,
And that cannot compare with music."

"Not so," say I. "Speech can move as well as music,
Ignite the spirit, kindle a fire that spreads to
Blood and bone. Indeed, is not the heart
The servant of the mind, being so moved?"

"Never a servant," you protest.
 "Say, instead, companion,
That moves the mind to action, from words alone.
The heart lifts logic to imagine greater worlds."

There is laughter in your voice,
And I abandon logic for the sweetness of the dusk
And the fire of my heart.
The dream goes misty, and,
Passing into sleep, comforted by your arms
And the moon above us both,
Do I feel my own wings sprout at last?

Warrior's Lament

The dawn is breaking cold and clear.
Silent now, and far too near,
The battlefield before me lies.
I gaze upon it with weary eyes,
I drain the dregs from Honor's cup
And watch the vultures at their sup...

And I think of all has passed me by
As Honor has dragged me here to die -
The lovers lost, the sights unseen,
Other people I might have been
Had I not chosen Honor's curse.
Of all my choices... that, the worst.

What good has Honor ever brought me?
Nay, I say She has only taught me
Deeper paths into how She caught me,
Trapped me, and brought me here.

For Honor's ways are harsh and old;
They say Fortune's favors fall to the bold,
But Honor sharpens a blade most cold,
And exacts a price most dear.

Across the field I see Her there:
Sunlight dapples Her raven hair,
And glows in Her sea-green eyes.
The knowing smile I most despise
Touches the bow of Her lovely lips...
She touches the sword at Her rounded hip.

"Arise, my hunter, and come away.
Over this field, Death now holds sway,
And you have business in other lands.
Come to me, take now My hands
And battle again in My name.
We will bet on another game."

And so I leave that field behind me,
With battle scars that still remind me...
I strive to throw off those chains that bind me,
And from that cold Queen retreat,

But still I contest the hordes of hell -
(Those foes who see Her face as well -
And that is the truth She will never tell)
As I kneel at Honor's feet.

Churchyard Yew

An ancient yew among the graves
Grows in that churchyard old.
And from behind it steps my love,
So dear and bright and bold.
"Arise, my lady, come away-
The looming night grows cold."
And so into the dark we walk,
Beneath bright stars above.

His eyes are wise and deep as ages
Past as they meet mine;
His fingers cold within my grasp
As our two hands entwine.
His cloak he wraps around me
As, beneath the moonlight's shine,
He kisses me...ah, Goddess bless,
His lips are rich as wine.

"December hastens to a close,
The Solstice now draws nigh...
The longest night the year will know.
Yet dawn will light the sky,
And morning come again, my love,
And hope and faith will rise,
And you will find another lord,
To gaze into your eyes...

"Another's love will ease your pain,
And brush away your tears,
And you will find another's arms
To shield you from your fears...
And I do bless you, o my love,
And bid you go from here -
For here I must remain, as I
Have done for this past year."

I pull the dagger from my belt,
Upon it, moonlight glows.
"I'll live no more without you, love.
For you must surely know
That many lives have bound us close,
And I will keep it so...
With you beneath that ancient yew
Is the sweetest home I know."

And when that ancient yew decays,
As Nature bids it do,
From that same bole new life will sprout,
Not only one... but two.
And our two hearts will grow as one,
The Tree of Life renewed,
As Death, transcended, frees us both
To love and learn anew.

Dark Moon, With Dancer

Clouded night, waning moon.
Fire at the circle's heart.
Drummers: clustered, laughing, then...
One beat, deep-voiced, steady,
The heart of the earth made manifest.
We breathe in once, then out... a second drum
Embroiders round the first,
And then a third, filling what space left open -
They call the blood to movement.

To the fire from the dark she comes -
The Dancer.
Neither young, nor old, fair nor plain,
For in this place between she is not herself,
But the Dance.

Slowly she begins, her fluid arms
Tell the tale she does not speak.
Tall as the sky, supple as reeds
In the wind, her body
Moves with serpents' grace,
Boneless - weightless -
Aloft on the drums' voices.
Her hips inform the orbits of the worlds.

Faster, spinning now,
One rhythm claims her feet
And, as she makes it hers,
The drummers play to her,
And she is theirs,
Yet still a queen apart.

Nor mortal flesh it seems can bind
This grace, this fire, this blaze
Of Goddess granting us Her Presence
And we are swaying as she
Draws the power down and through her,
Blessing those who drum
And those who sway
And those whose tears
Are given to Her glory and the Earth
That holds us all...

She slows, and slow the drums subside
Until that heartbeat just remains,
Then softens down to silence.
As from a trance we wake and
She is smiling as we praise her,
And she is now our friend,
But still a Queen.

Horned Crown

We'd been all day out hunting,
My brother Llew and I :
With ease, our spears had slain the boar,
And swift our shafts did fly!

But we were late returning.
The sun was setting low,
And we still deep within the woods,
With a mile or more to go...

    Chorus:

    And He who wears the Horned Crown
    Will lead the Hunt by night,
    And many the fools in wood and field
    That flee from Them in fright...

We hurried through the tangled brush
But all to no avail:
Behind, we heard the Hunt's white hounds
Come howling on our trail.

Their ghostly forms, with blood-red ears,
Rushed at us through the gloom.
But Those who rode behind the hounds -
With Them did ride our doom.

(Chorus)

Upon a snorting, red-eyed beast,
The Lord of that Wild Ride
Came thundering through the darkling wood
With His band on every side.

And grim, and proud, and fell was He
Who wore that horned crown,
And an awful smile did scar His face
As upon us He looked down...

"Ye've strayed too far a-hunting, lads,
And now the price is due:
For one of you must come with us."
And He pointed, then, at Llew.

"I think it's ye must pay the price,
And fealty to Us swear:
In all this fey, Unseelie horde
There'll be none half as rare!"

(Chorus)

I pulled my keen sword singing free,
To my brother's side I sprang:
"To take my kin, first go through me!"
Through that glade grim laughter rang.

And the Lord of all that dark brigade
Drew steel and came for me,
Blade red as blood in the dying sun
As we fought beneath the trees...

Until, at last, I ran Him through-
We had battled to the death.
To the ground He sank. These words He spoke
With His last faltering breath:

"Ye've bested me full fair," He said,
"And your brother's life ye've won.
But now my place belongs to ye,
To do as I have done.

"For the Balance must be kept," He said,
Between the Dark and Light;
And all souls face within themselves
The Wild Hunt in the night."

  And now, I wear that Horned Crown
  And lead the Hunt by night,
  And many the fools in wood and field
  That flee from us in fright.

Year's End: The Traveler's Tale

Year's end comes rushing now,
The dark falls sooner, stays long and longer,
And the night air is thick with frost, even in these sunlit lands.
I am a traveler here, and do not know the customs.

Were I where they knew me best,
The long hall would be alive with children's laughter,
Dogs by the fire snapping over bones.
Busy, yes, always busy... harvests to gather in,
The herd beasts to harvest and preserve, salted or dried
And what the huntsmen bring, against the coming of the snow...
Clothing to prepare, to mend, or make,
And the house to clean and freshen.

But of an evening, there is time for all to gather
At the great table and share the bounty.
We stand on no ceremony here. None sit below the salt.
All are welcome, and all are family.
We eat with gratitude, and the wine and beer flow
As freely as we may, to celebrate this coming together.
By my side, my merry wife presides over all,
Her bright eyes and flushed cheeks more beauty
In one place than the world deserves.

In my sleep I stir, restless,
Pull the blankets up around me, my spirit lost
In dreaming. A strange bed, in these foreign lands.
I am a traveler here, and do not know the customs.

And when the stranger comes, he is made welcome,
For that is the law of my land: to all is the open hand
Given and received in kind. We are a gentle people here,
Though hardy and fearless. We will let none wander in the dark
To die alone and afraid. A comely man, tall and dark,

Well-spoken, not from here, but polite - I lead him to the table,
And welcome is given him, food and drink, he smiles
And kisses my lady's hand as she greets him...

As the door is burst asunder, and men flood in, ten
Then twenty and the fire flashes on their long steel blades,
And our weapons are not among us at the table where we dine.
And the children, screaming, slaughtered as
                                    the dogs are slaughtered,
And my men among them with daggers, so brave, so fearless,
Dying nonetheless - the women, shrieking, then silent,
And I am screaming as I attack, I throw myself at my wife
And that comely stranger but too late, too late by half...

As her hair in his fist holds her helpless and his bright dagger
Arcs across her throat, and she falls back against me and
I lunge as he strikes again, blood flows and I know no more...
I travel toward the Light, as is our custom....

And then awake. The charnel house is ice around me,
The fires gone out and all is death and silent as the night...
The smell of blood in all the air and she is staring sightless
Into my bleary eyes, and the pain... the pain... the pain...
Somehow I rise, and bind my wound-
                              how not mortal I cannot fathom -
And then I find the brooch upon the floor beside her, fallen
From her cold fingers' nerveless grasp,
                                    the brooch that stranger wore.
And I depart into the endless night, that talisman beside my heart.

To search. To travel all those lands of legend that before
Were only children's tales and the dreams of drunken men,
Until that arcane brooch - that froth of filigree and gems that now
Is all that matters in my world –
                        revealed to me the hand that gave it birth,
And where he dwells. I have come across a dozen worlds of woe
With but one goal, to the ruin of all I was and will become –
to find the man who stripped me of my love,
                    my life and all who knew me best...
And bear him with me down into
                    the endless night that holds my heart.

And world's end comes rushing now,
My dagger plunges deep, and his heart sunders
and then mine own...the night takes my last breath.
I travel with the night, to where I know the customs.

CHAPTER FIVE

ARCANA

Fool

The world behind you,
Wisdom nipping at your heels,
Dare you take that step?

Magician

Bones of pure will dreamed...
Made manifest on solid
Shores of love and blood.

High Priestess

Between dark and light,
The veil lifts - she speaks to you,
 Hidden worlds revealed.

Empress

Fields, bodies, minds grow.
From her womb creation flows,
And all thrive in peace.

Emperor

Unbending Power,
Your throne is stable and strong -
Care for those you rule.

Hierophant

Power channeled through
The structures of the world: we
Make traditions ours.

Lovers

What we believe of
Love lies between heart and mind...
The balance is truth.

Chariot

Go faster, faster!
Balance must be restored first -
Focused is swifter.

Strength

Persevere. Gently
Close the Lion's mouth. True strength
Softly moves mountains

Hermit

My light in darkness,
A beacon for others, is
My quest for wisdom.

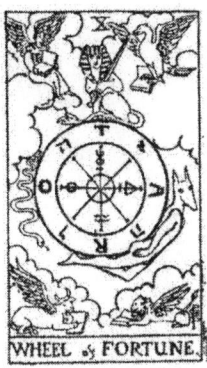

Wheel

Spinning, some fall down,
Others rise up... the Wheel whirls
Us all through our lives.

Justice

She is not blind now.
We get what we deserve as
She holds high her scales...

Hanged Man

Inaction is choice.
Perspective is everything...
What do you see now?

Death

We shed this life as
Snakes shed skins: to grow, and change,
And brighten, renewed.

Temperance

Inner and outer,
Body, soul, actions are one.
Balance is achieved.

Devil

The daemon lover
Promises all : flesh and blood
Exalt o'er spirit.

Tower

Lightning strikes us all.
Raze failing foundations to
Build yourself better.

Star

Trust in yourself.
Trust the stars to guide you home.
Trust your heart to hope.

Moon

She lights the Darkness.
Reflecting the truth's harsh glare,
She speaks more subtly.

Sun

Sun breaks through the clouds.
Light, warmth, love, all you want of
What your soul needs most...

Judgement

With all else gone, we
Rise from what's held us down and
Learn where we'll go next.

World

You have it all now...
Rest a bit. But not for long:
New Worlds call the Fool.

CHAPTER SIX

NEVER AGAIN THE BURNING

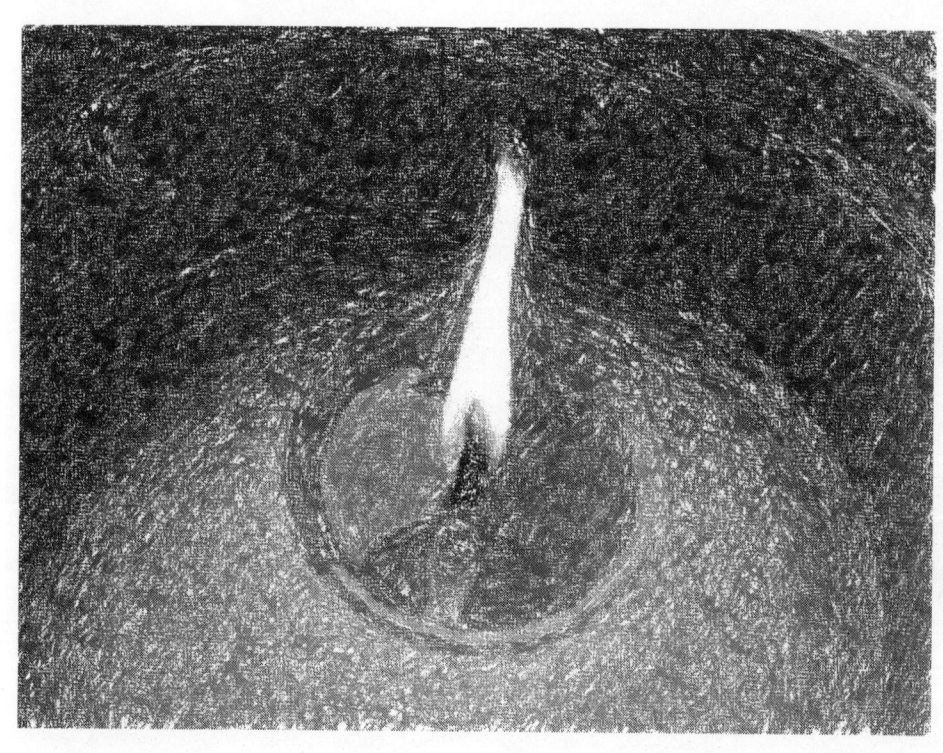

Never Again the Burning

In the dream
It is always the morning of my execution...

... I know they will come today.
Last night the jailer, pulling up his trousers, sneered
"Perhaps you'll fancy the pole
They give you in the morning more than mine,
Stubborn bitch."

I think
He liked it better when I had strength
And spirit enough to fight him.
He is too stupid to lie, just to torment me.
I will welcome death, though the dying scares me.

I was a healer - how long ago? oh, Gods,
I cannot think straight any more...
And I know that these gross insults
To my body will never mend.
The pain is constant, and they have sworn me
I will go to the fire conscious and aware.
My Goddess, I am sick to my soul with shame;
At the last I gave them screaming what they wanted,
Mouthed any obscenity they asked, told them
What they told me to say.
My sanity remains only because your names
Go with me to the pyre, and to the grave beyond,
And only there.
Oh, beloved, if I could only see you one last time,
That your clean spirit's fire
Could rid me of this filth and fear...

The crowd gathers now.
I hear them outside, laughing, festive -
Gods grant I will be entertaining enough.
I wonder if those pious souls who in the past

Have asked my help will mourn me?
Well, I shall be glad to quit this stinking cell.
The rats grow bolder as I decline...
Oh, Mother, give me strength!

I hear the guards outside:
"What," I taunt them, "three of you,
All for one small, half-starved wench?
Indeed, terrible I must be!"
They have the grace to look ashamed,
The youngest one grown pale and horrified
At the sight of me; I delivered his wife
Of a fine strong son not many weeks ago,
But now I dare not ask him how the child fares.
"Nay, you must carry me or drag me,
My fine bravos - I fear I have danced too long
With your good priest in his fine Spanish boots."
They haul me to my feet, and the pain....
But I will not scream again for their amusement!

I must go naked, then, to my death before these fools?
I would not have them see me so, who danced
Naked for the Goddess, graceful and free,
Without a trace of shame.
Their avaricious eyes defile me,
As their twisted priests defiled my body's temple.

There are many strangers here in the square,
Priests and villagers from all the country round...
I am to be a marvelous, far-felt lesson, I see.

They bind me to their stake, too tight, more agony,
The splintering pole claws my raw back,
My shoulders wrenched and cramping, the rough rope
Burning my wrists. My legs will not support me.
I sag in my bonds, and I fill slowly with terror,
Like a pitcher with muddy water.
A priest approaches - oh, Goddess, must I suffer them even now?
The crowd protests the cup in his hands.

He exhorts them gently:
His sect bears mercy toward all,
Malice toward none, and might not even such as I
Be saved at the bitter end?
I don't know this one. I fight to raise my head,
To spit in his face, for one last show of defiance...

Mother of All, NO! Not you, not here...
How have you come here, beloved
To trade your green robes for their black,
Your antlered crown for their cross?
Surely I dream, I dream...
But now I smell your clean scent
And your dear presence cloaks me in peace.
Rage fires in your eyes, but your pure love
Sustains me, strengthens and warms me.
You brush the hair back from my face.
The cup you hold to my bruised lips I gave you
At our handfasting...
Softly you whisper, "Drink deep of salvation, my dear love,"
And your voice, harsh with unshed tears,
Rips at my soul and my own tears begin, and fully
I drink of your deep eyes and the chalice,
And the taste of the flying herbs bursts on my tongue,
Belladonna, aconite, dark sweet dreams...

They are coming now, with the fire.
Almost you linger too long, haunted eyes on mine,
But as sleep steals over me I see you melt safely into the throng.
I am drifting now. I hear my mother singing, far away -
Strange, she has been dead these many years.
The pain is gone. I am a little girl again, I am safe,
My mother is calling me, and I run gladly to her arms.
Back in the room I have left behind, someone has been careless
With the supper, Mother - they must turn the spit faster,
For I can smell the roasting meat burning,
And the dinner guests are shouting.....

I wake in cold sweat, and cannot drink
From the glass you bring me. Oh, sisters and brothers, hear!
Our daughters, our sons, must not dream these dreams!
We must defend ourselves, stand with each other
And make the arsonists Let. Us. Be.
Oh, my kinfolk, hear: never again,
Never again the burning.

(Author's note: This piece, written in 1985, has stood my personal test of time in most of its wording. I have, for this edition, changed the last verse to include those beloved kinsmen I have found over the years... it is not just my sisters to whom the task falls, to keep our children and ourselves safe from those who still would do us harm, whether physical, spiritual, or legal.

Let us stand together. There is no place for "witch wars" in this day and age. If we will not help each other, how can we ever help ourselves?

The title of this piece is taken, with permission, from the late P.E.I. Bonewits' "Aquarian Manifesto".)

Magick

"Magick?" she said softly,
Her hair gleaming, her eyes
Shining in the fire's dance.
"We all have magick.
But in some folks, it runs
Closer to the surface. And with it,
We weave the old rhythms.
The voice of the Earth Mother sings in our ears.
We feel the Horned Presence peering sunlit
Through the trees. We feel the Lady's grace
In the night wind, in the glow of the Moon.
Magick?" and she shook her head,
"Magick is the tease. Power is the drawing card.
But once the Path is taken, true hearts
Learn the wisdom of the inner ways,
The many paths to the center.
There is no greater magick than to find
The source of all Creation within yourself.
It is not spells, and enchantments,
Potions, or powders, graveyards and bat wings.
Magick," and her cat stirred, purred,
Green eyes wide and ancient as her Lady's,
"True magick is the balance of the soul.
It lies within us all...
And the Way is open."

Pagan's Way

Not for my feet the high golden road:
My heart is set in silver,
Wind in the trees,
Green grass beneath my feet,
And the moonlit grove.
Content with the power
In the deep bones of the Earth Mother,
I would not control the heavens.

I have trod the solitary path,
And will again.
I have heard the Lady's laughter at moonrise
And suffered Her tender scourge in my heart.
I have feasted with the Lord of Shadows,
And been reborn.

I have spied shy horned faces peering, golden-eyed,
From the rocks at the circle's edge.
I have called to the Watchers at the world's four quarters,
And from Their gates, They answered...
I have watched the salamanders in the fire's embers,
And the undines in the chortling stream.

All this I know, and more.
I have no need of the passionate cold of the celestial vault,
Or the comet's fire.
I will walk my quiet road in peace,
And conjure spiral wonders -
For the morning sun is gold enough for me.

Matters of Life and Death

Came Death one morning early to Greenwood,
To speak with the Healer there.
Death was a lord both dark and tall,
And wondrous, terrible fair.

Said He, "We've striven, you and I,
Over some who approached My door.
But I find you pagans fear Me less
Than most I've seen before.
Can you tell me why this is? " He asked,

And the Healer, laughing, replied,
"Because, my Lord, we pagans know
That we can return when we die.

You're the other half of Life," she said.
"No less, but nothing more...
And all the lives must come, in time,
To wait outside Your door.
But I heal, my Lord, in my Lady's name,
And it's She who guides my hand,
That none I love will walk,
Before their time, Your shadowed land.
And all that falls shall rise again:
I know this to be true.
But none whose lives I hold in trust
Shall early come to You."

Death smiled then, and took His leave.
The Healer stayed, and found
A single pomegranate seed
Beside her on the ground.
She planted it. And in the spring,
When she returned to see
If anything had grown, she found
A slender apple tree....

Dark Hecate's Hounds

See the man who flees so swiftly,
Glancing often back in fright?
Dark Hecate's hounds are belling,
Coursing prey in the dead of night...

Suddenly She stands before him,
Pack of shadows at Her side,
Silent tide of blackness swelling,
Gleaming fangs and feral eyes.

"Dream of darkness, stay your slayers
Furred and fanged, of fearsome mien!
Why do you pursue Your servant?
I, your slave have always been!

"Always I have sought the Goddess,
Praised Her names both far and near.
Always I have tried to find Her
In the ones I would hold dear.

"Is it my fault I have not found Her,
Only women, weak and frail
Who had within no trace of glory?
My sorrow grows each time I fail!

"But still I seek, and still I praise Her!
What have I done, that You pursue?"
Now he dares frown at Hecate.
"How, then, have I angered You?"

Now Hecate's rage surrounds him,
Smothers him in icy wind.
Now Her flaming eyes impale him
As Her voice invades his mind:

"Fool! You have left behind you
Scores of women in your dust -
Betrayed by you and your illusions,
Hapless victims of your lust!

"And one of these was My disciple."
Now he flinches as She smiles.
"She you left alone, and dying
As she fought to bear your child.

"When she died, your name she whispered,
Curses murmured like a prayer.
She sorrowed only for her child,
That she had not the strength to bear.

"The child's soul I took unto Me,
Gave it peace in the Summerland.
Her, I gave the boon she begged for:
See? Beside me here, she stands!"

Now one clot of shadow shimmers,
Shifting shape before his eyes:
Fair and mournful is the woman
Who puts off the hound's disguise.

Terror battles lust within him.
Suddenly the terror wins
As out she stretches silken arms
And bares white teeth in feral grin.

"Come to me, my sweet," she whispers,
"Come to me - oh, long and long
It has been since last you held me,
But my love for you is strong.

"I never died, although my body
 Passed away into the dust -
 Come to me! See how betrayal
 Taught me how to love and trust!"

Now he turns, in panic screaming,
No avail - a hound again,
His lost love leaps, her white fangs gleaming,
And his body lies there, slain.

Now from the corpse his spirit rises,
Now Hecate's laughter rings.
"Mortal fool, now run your fastest!
Close behind my children sing.

"At your heels, forever find them!
This the boon she asked of me:
From her touch you'd not escape,
No matter where or how you flee."

See the man that runs so swiftly,
Staring often back in fright -
Dark Hecate's hounds are belling,
Coursing prey in the dead of night....

CHAPTER SEVEN

FIVE WORDS FOR LOVE

Heart

What's to think about?
Love rules my heart for my sake,
My mind must follow....

Breaking

Feel my heart, breaking-
Hear pieces crashing on your
Mute indifference.

Dreams

Cold, blackwater Night
Flows around me. Sleepless, I
Weep for gentler dreams.

Storm

The wind howls outside.
I am restless and bereft -
My heart howls for you.

Silence

If a perfect world,
I would already know what
Silence parts us now...

Dawning

If the world still stands
By tomorrow's dawning light,
Will I find you, Love?

Darkness

Darkness has my back...
when the cold sun comes, my heart
Will stay with the night

Oya

Oya, Queen of Change,
Your storms sweep my cluttered life
Clear of old mistakes.

Rise

Today my heart hurts.
I light a candle and wait
For my soul to rise...

Spiral

walking the spiral.
small steps in to the center.
back out is harder.

Now

Bravery is slow.
Persistence is somewhat more
Attainable now...

Five Words For Love

And in that quiet moment,
Between beats of your heart...
Between words that don't work,
Between thoughts that don't count,
Between moments that won't fade
Decently as the real world
Insists they should...

That quiet moment stretches out
Until, in that eternity of time,
You know the five words for love
The ancients knew.
The five words that fold into themselves
All you never knew to say before,
With the paucity of meaning one poor word allows.

Like the five elements that compose the cosmos.
Revealed to you are all the spokes of the wheel,
And all the roads to the center, and all
The mysteries of the human heart, so lost,
So broken, so brave that it can rise
From the ashes like the Phoenix
Burning...and find the sky.

TempusBound Publishing
2013

Made in the USA
Charleston, SC
24 July 2013